Faith Works

Charles E. Pratt, Jr

ISBN:1497448751
ISBN-13:9781497448759

DEDICATION

This work is dedicated to my wife, Evelyn Judy Pratt, to my children, Lisa, Tonya, Terry, and Charles(III), my late friend, & cousin; Bishop Joseph B. Hargo, my Victory Temple Church family, and the greater family of believers.

Acknowledgements

This book could not have been written without the time , suggestions, guidance, and support from numerous people. I humbly say, "Thank you " from the depths of my heart.

To our friend, and expert in literary work; Mrs. Betel Arnold. Your persistence to see us stay on task, have helped bring us to this reality.

To my wife, Evelyn, who has worked tireless hours, assisting in so many ways. I truly appreciate you in so many ways. You have been my rock.

Charles E. Pratt, Jr.

FOREWARD TO *FAITH WORKS*

I've known Rev. Pratt for eleven years as the result of his service on the Board of Trustees for the Berkshire Athenaeum overseeing my work there, as the Library Director. He is a thoughtful and pragmatic presence at our monthly meetings where he brings his gentle sense of humor and kindness, but there's tremendous passion below the surface. Rev. Pratt has traveled all over the country as a preacher, evangelist, and inspirational speaker, so passion is no stranger; and that's what we see, in *Faith Works,* the very personal, first person mix of biographical anecdotes, poetry, essays, and scripture designed to inspire readers, to define and explain faith, and to clearly demonstrate that "Faith works." Prepare to be moved because the scriptural affirmations contained in this book are designed to develop a powerful new mindset, to actively lead you to positive, life-changing outcomes.

Ronald Latham, Director

Berkshire Athenaeum, Pittsfield's Public Library

Pittsfield, Massachusetts

Supt. Charles E. Pratt Jr. is a walking, breathing, living, testimony of; *Faith Works.* Do you have the faith to move mountains? Do you have the faith to believe the impossible is possible? What about the faith to fulfill your dreams? If you do not, *this book is for you.* In a powerful and poetic narrative, Supt. Charles E. Pratt Jr., shares nuggets from his own life story to illustrate how vital faith is for any victory. Keep this book by your side anytime the enemy wages war. Your faith will not fail you—*Faith Works.*

A must-read for every believer! —

Betel Arnold,

Author, speaker, talk-show host

Springfield, Massachusetts

From personal experience, the author provides an easy to read road map to those facing uncertainty and doubt in their faith-walk and travels. In a nutshell, FAITH WORKS for travelers that simply utilize a GPS (God's Plan for Salvation)!

When our faith in GOD tends to faint or stagger, God in His own special way sends a faith uplifting message our way. I was in the middle of feeling so down and out for being unemployed for so long. And in today's mail, I opened a big brown envelope to find Brother Pratt's book, Faith Works.

And after reading Faith Works through, I eventually received what Rev. Pratt calls a Faith-lift just at the right time and not a second late! And GOD is never late! When Jesus finally arrived at Lazarus funeral, He was four days late, but He was still on time!

Sincerely:

Clifford Sanderson,

Educator, Author,

Winnipeg, Manitoba, Canada

~~~~~~

Faith works. Faith. Works; Each alone, a simple word, but together they form a profound message of inspiration; of purpose; of hope.

Faith is the cornerstone of the community built in our hearts and lives on a foundation of unity, compassion, honor, courage, fidelity, comfort, strength, and resolution.

Faith works. Trust and believe...

Faith Works written by Reverend Charles Pratt, Jr., who with his wife Evelyn Pratt, has devoted his life to the teachings of the Lord, the prophets of love, and most especially, the tenets of faith, has captured the awesome elements of this message in his book.

Gianna Allentuck
Adjustment Counselor, Elias Brookings Elementary School,
Member, Mayor's Citywide Violence Prevention Task Force
Springfield, Massachusetts
~~~~~~~~~~~~~~~~~~~~~~~~~

The Reverend Charles E Pratt, Jr. is a minister of the gospel of Jesus Christ and the Pastor of Victory Temple Church of God in Christ in Pittsfield, Massachusetts, and I have known him for over 30 years to be a man who is well balanced, and is devoted to right interpretation of Scriptures. I have followed his ministry closely for all these years with great satisfaction.

I am very honored and privileged, to write a foreword for this work by Reverend Charles Pratt on the subject of *"FAITH WORKS."* Reverend Pratt is in an unenviable position to write on this topic. *Why you may ask?* Because as you read this treatise of his, you will find out he is not writing from a position of theory, but from a practical experience with God. To quote one wise man who said *"A man with an experience is never at the mercy of a man, with a theory or an argument."*

Reverend Pratt is a prolific writer, *and "FAITH WORKS"* is just one of the many books he has written and published over the years. I am in possession of many and have always been blessed in reading them. In *"FAITH WORKS"* he has made it clear to us how *Biblical faith works*. There are a lot of books on the subject of "faith" out in the Christian marketplace however; many people are left be-wildered and discouraged after reading them. No so with this treatise.

Reverend Pratt has once again made clear, that what God has given to us in the Scriptures is not a set of *"pat answers"* whereby, we snap our fingers in some *"mystical way"* that is based on some *"esoteric understanding"* of God and of the Scriptures, in that we can obtain some *"magical answer"* the way lightning flashes.

On the subject of **"FAITH"** Scripture is quite clear that we cannot please God without it. It is also true that those that lived by **faith,** did so in a very *"practical way,"* we might say in *"down to earth"* illustrations that can be applied to our everyday lives.

I would highly recommend this book to any person who is honestly interested in living the life of **"faith that works"** without which it is impossible to please God.

Dr. Austin K. Smith

Professor and Ordaining Director of:

Rhema Studies of Theology Association

Pastor of Toronto Gospel Lighthouse

Toronto, Ontario, Canada

December 2015

What is the significance of Faith? It's the...assurance of the reality of things hoped for..." (Heb. 11:1). Supt. Pratt carefully examines and succinctly reflects on the multifaceted nature of faith. Because of its crucial role in the believer's relationship with God through Christ—"Without Faith it is impossible to please Him." The reader's spiritual maturity will be greatly enhanced through the reading of this book. Pastor Pratt draws from an extensive background of faith encountering personal experiences, that bring authenticity to his writing. I do believe that all who read "Faith Works" will be truly blessed.

Humbly Summited,

Dr. Bryant Robinson, Jr.
Juristictional Prelate of Greater Massachusetts Juristiction of the Church of God in Christ

Pastor of First Church (Fitchburg, MA & Macedonia Church of God in Christ (Springfield, MA)

Former: Supreintendent of Springfield Public Schools &
Dean of Cambridge College (Springfield, MA)
~~~~~~~~~~~~~~~~~~~~~~~~~~~~

Charles E. Pratt, Jr.

Contents

Introduction………………………………………….. 7

1. What Is Faith……………………………………. 9

2. Matter of Fact…………………………………. 13

    When Faith is in Practice…………………… 17

    What Faith Does…………………………….. 18

3. Feet Behind Faith……………………………… 19

4. Diligence………………………………………… 23

5. Faith Works and Doesn't Doubt……………… 25

6. From Milk to Meat……………………………… 29

7. Faith Works Through Love…………………… 33

8. When Faith is Applied………………………… 35

9. Application for Situation……………………… 37

    More Than a Conquer…………………………. 42

10. The Walk Exceeding the Talk……………… 43

The 'From To' of Faith.................................. 48

Faith Always Works.................................... 49

Keep Keeping On 50

We Faithful.. 51

11. High Praise Stirs High Faith...................... 53

Growing Faith... 58

Giving Love... 59

Faithful in God's Word............................... 60

Why Not More Than.................................. 61

Faith is All in All..................................... 63

A Faith Lift... 64

Practice Faith... 65

The Devil Comes...................................... 67

Heaven's Blessings................................... 68

Faith Builds.. 70

I Shan't Recant...................................... 72

It's a New Day.. 73

Discover the Counterfeiter...................... 74

My Faith... 76

Hold On and Let Go............................... 78

12. Success and Blessings............................... 79

13. Speaking of Seeking.................................. 81

Faith Works....................................... 84

When Faith is Applied........................... 86

Faith Over all..................................... 88

14. Faith and Fruit..................................... 91

15. The Attitude of Faith.............................. 93

16. Existence and Persistence 95

17. Working Faith 97

18. Ever Ready Faith 103

19. The Face of Faith 105

20. From Dependence to Transcendence 113

21. Don't Stop, Don't Quit 117

22. Effectual Prayer 119

23. Turn Aside 123

24. What Faith Isn't 125

25. Our Bible 127

26. Understanding the Bible 131

27. On the Money 133

28. The Miracle of the Money.................... 139

29. Attack Your Lack................................... 143

Compulsive Behavior 152

Exorbitant.. 153

Faith Is... 154

Which Do You Want............................. 156

For Money.. 157

Money Makes....................................... 158

Find Your 'Niche'................................. 160

Building A Nest Egg............................. 161

On Paying Tithes................................. 162

Invest in the Church............................ 164

Money.. 165

Giving... 166

For the Love of Money............................. 168

8 Turns on Faith 170

Thoughts\ Reflections 171

30. Conclusion 175

* indented titles are; Poems

Charles E. Pratt, Jr.

Introduction

"Even so faith if it hath not works, is dead, being alone." JAMES 2:17

Faith works, here are two short words, so precise, practical, and very powerfully productive. **Faith Works,** not just a saying but a doing.

I am a living witness to the fact that faith works. I have devoted deep thought and consideration to the subject, faith works. I preach it, I teach it, and I testify to it. Faith can be found both working and workable. In other words, as you work your faith, your faith works for you. You do and faith will too!

In the following pages I will share a few profound things concerning **Faith Works**. It is my earnest prayer that your faith will grow to obtaining the promises of scripture and claiming the blessings God wants you to have.

Don't be timid or so easily frightened. Take hold of faith, Bible-believing faith, and let it work to improve your health, prosperity, and overall wealth.   Come to know that you know for yourself, Faith Works!

Charles Edward Pratt Jr.

1.

What Is Faith

Hebrews 11; 6

"But without faith it is impossible to please Him! For he that commeth to God must believe that he is , and that He is a rewarder of them that diligently seek Him."

What is faith? Faith is seeking after the will and purpose of God for your life. The hymnologist said, *"Where He leads me I will follow, I'll go with Him all the way."* So faith is a journey in the directions that He, God would send you.

Verse #7 says, by faith, Noah...moved with fear prepared an ark.

#8 says, by faith Abraham...obeyed and went out, not knowing whither he went.

#9 says by faith, he so journed in the Land of Promise, as in a strange country, dwelling in Tabernacles with Isaac and Jacob the heirs with Him of the same promise. Faith dares to step out and move in the direction of the promise, the hope, and the dream.

Faith, trust in God's Word. Faith believes He meant what He said, and said what He meant, that He, God will bring it to pass.

Numbers 23; 19 says: *God is not a man that He should lie, neither the son of man that He should repent: Hath He said and shall He not do it? Or hath He spoken, and shall He not make it good?*

Trusting, believing, receiving the scriptures speak of the power of prayer-the power of the Word of God, Overall the power, of your faith in God.

God deals in addition and multiplication while the devil deals in subtraction and division. The enemy comes to bring you down, while Christ comes to build you up, to build your faith.

Many in the world would view your faith as an abstraction, something made up in a mental or mind game that we in the church play. Never mind the scientific, the metaphysical or the philosophical here. Let's quickly simplify the fact of faith from the fantasy of fiction. Let's look at faith from a Biblical standard, which we can well understand. Bible faith when biblically and properly applied to our life situations, always works. Simple believing makes for simply receiving.

2.

Matter of Fact

Bible faith, simple believing, and simply receiving is not mind over matter but it's a matter of fact. It wasn't mind over matter that allowed Jesus Christ to walk on the water, but it was a matter of fact that He did walk on the water, fact on top of fact is a stack of facts. Add them, subtract them, multiply, or divide them, you still come up with the facts.

God calls us to trust in the truth of His Word. We are to step out and move in the direction of His promise. Faith doesn't just talk, It also walks. It's more than an oath or saying, "I believe." You have to do something kinetic about your believing in God. **Whenever God says go**, you go and **whenever God says wait**, you wait, and **whatever God tells you to do**, you do.

"They that wait upon the Lord shall renew their strength; they shall mount up on wings as eagles. They shall run and not be weary, and they shall walk and not faint." Isaiah 40:31

No, we don't faint at the size or scope of the task that's in front of us. Faith is that God will make a way for you to do what He told you, living right, walking right, or talking right, going to LA if that's where He told you to go.

I say, "Faith isn't mind over matter but faith is a matter of fact." The astonishing fact of faith therefore is that faith is a matter of fact. Faith should be simple, easy to deal with, not complicated though very profound   Jesus spoke of having childlike faith; *"But Jesus called them unto him, and said, "Suffer little children to come unto me, and forbid them not: for of such is the kingdom of God. Verily I say unto you, whosoever shall not receive the kingdom of God as a little child shall in no wise enter there in."*   Luke 18:16-17

Faith need not to be intense and scientific. Faith is not a manner of mathematical logic or the explicative matrix of something far beyond our grasp. The application of faith doesn't require a Ph.D. Degree or a celebrated fancy formula of sorts.

"Now faith is the substance of things hoped for, the evidence of things not seen." Heb. 11:1

Faith is the glue that holds creation together; it is the matter of fact that allows the mathematician and the physicist to postulate. However, faith is deeply spiritual; it rests on and pertains to our sacred sense of fundamental trust in God. It's about basic believing, it must be very personal. Faith relates to the relationship we have with God. I simply confide in him, I believe that He can, He will and He is doing or going to do all that He has promised to do. I believe God!

I am more into the expectation of my miracle than the explanation of my miracle; my concern isn't so much how God does what he does, when he does it, but that he does it. Never mind the how so but rather thank you Jesus for the know so! I charge it to my application of faith when the way is made or the door is open, I'll not speculate as to the methodology of God who picked up nothing and made something. No need

For analysis, evaluation, and attempted organization. Jesus said it, God did it, I believe it and that settles it. And that is a matter of fact!

When Faith is in Practice

No need to worry though Satan attack us,

Serene is the scene when faith is in practice.

Remember old Job in the midst of attack.

He trusted God in spite of his lack.

Turn from whatever would cause you to scare.

Take hold of faith and handle with care.

Doubt is dejected when faith is elected.

Delegate faith and you will be protected.

Faith when applied unravels the unbelief.

It undresses distress and brings in relief.

What Faith Does

Faith Turns a Retreat

Into an Advance

Creates An Enhance

At Every Chance.

Faith Enlarges the Small

Endorses the Call

Faith Reinforces All In All.

3.

Feet behind Faith

"Now the Lord had said unto Abram, get thee out of thy country, and from thy kindred, and from thy house into a land that I will shew thee." Genesis 12; 1

You have to get your feet behind your faith. Be more than willing to do some walking. You will see faith at work and working; when the talk of faith becomes the walk of faith. Here's the powerful prerequisite for a move or miracle from God, you have to do something, the ball is in your court, so dare to take a shot.

How did you get started? How did you get all those open doors? How did you meet all those big shots? How's come you got picked to be Keynote speaker? Like the song says; "I've been a lot of places, and I've seen a lot of faces." I've had the opportunity to speak in many huge conventions, conduct revival in many mega churches, and appear on national and international TV talk shows.

All of this I must say is nothing more than a walk of faith. Faith works and Jesus never fails. From day one till today, my faith has and continues to work. Our first evangelistic tour was no cake walk but definitely a walk of faith. I remember when all those "Deep People" were prophesying and telling me I should quit my job at the research center and go full time on the road. When I did quit my job, and go out preaching, those folks were nowhere to be found. Their money was not where their mouth was. Nobody helped us.

I had sent out some letters, by faith, letting pastors know I was on the road for Jesus, available for *meetings*. A return came, inviting us to Miami, Florida

The car was an issue. We would be blessed to get to Delaware, Delaware, Ohio that is. It was only twenty five miles down the road, let alone 1200 miles to Miami. I found out then, that when God opens a door, faith in God, makes a way. We started out by faith. We didn't procrastinate. Procrastination: *to put off doing something until a future time; to postpone or defer taking action.* Procrastination can be the worst enemy of faith, causing you to sit in the seat of doing nothing, at a standstill, in a stalemate, going nowhere.

Working faith, does not procrastinate, it doesn't put off, but it puts on. It puts on the *armour of God*, and takes on doubt, skepticism, and unbelief. Faith says I can, I will, and I am. Yes, I am able to do all things through Christ. Ephesians 6; 10, 11 says; *"Finally my brethren, be strong in the Lord, and in the power of His might. Put on the whole armour of God that ye may be able to stand against the wiles of the devil."* So we put our war clothes on and took off for Miami, Florida. Judy and I with our little girl Lisa, I preached my way to Florida, and the Holy Ghost, opened doors every mile of the way. The fact, that I was broke, turned out to be a blessing. I preached in Cincinnati, Atlanta, Jacksonville, and finally Miami, Florida. A circuit was opened up that I can travel today, friends were met, and miracles happened- faith worked.

Faith continues to work; it is the machine that brings believing into receiving, causing us to realize every hope and every dream. Faith works, like the carpenter's tool box, all complete with hammer and saw. We just need to do some cutting, hammering, and some putting together. Then again faith works, like the auto mechanics diagnostic equipment. You find out what's wrong; what's in need of repair. Faith troubleshoots, gets answers, comes to conclusions, and finds the way, faith works. When we as believers will allow our faith to work for us, there is no telling what the results. Great miracles are bound to occur. Working faith will over and over confirm the fact of Holy Writ.

"God is our refuge and strength, a very present help in trouble." Psalm 46:1

"He that comes to God must believe that He is and that He is a rewarder of them that diligently seek Him." Hebrews 11: 6

4.

Diligence

Diligence speaks of constant careful effort, perseverance, the keep on keeping on, that will to look into the face of a storm and say, I still believe God. Praise the Lord anyhow! So diligence is therefore the calling card for faith. I'm talking about that painstaking attention and careful examination we give to know what God is calling us to do. You need to choose the right direction. Know which road to take. Understand the proper mode of transportation for getting to where you want to go.

Be willing to put your feet behind your faith, working faith is at work, when the talk starts to walk. It has been said, "The problem with people is people." Abraham was called away from his family and kin folks. Abraham, the *Father of Faith*, had to get away from the advice of people in order to heed the advice of God. Abraham got up and got going. Often, our family and friends can be the greatest hindrance in our *faith walk.*

5.

Faith Works and Doesn't Doubt

Be assured that faith works and doesn't doubt. Faith knows for sure that unbelieving is unacceptable! "Without faith it is impossible to please God." In the midst of your midnight, hold on until morning. Faith works to bring in brightest light. Faith works in the tightest place displacing difficulty and determining God's will and purpose, God's plan, and God's place.

Faith works, so let it work to change every negative situation in your life. So, we are going from seeming bad to seeing good. Yes, seeing through the eyes of faith. In the light of working faith, every load is lighter and every burden is brighter!

In the midst of the hungry lion's den, faith

works. Ole Brother Daniel will testify. Faith works to make the most dangerous lion docile.

I remember well, being guest singers at a Full Gospel Convention in Dayton, Ohio. We sang the song, *"How big is God."* The power of God came down and the people rejoiced. When wife and I went back to our seats, a brother came up to me saying, "You should go to Winnipeg." He handed me the card of a pastor in Winnipeg, Manitoba, a place I had never been and had no intentions of going. I took the card; put it on my desk in Columbus where it stayed for weeks. From time to time, I would pick that card up and read:

Evangelistic Tabernacle,

Pastor Ray Bradley,

Ellis and Burnell, Winnipeg, Manitoba .

Early one Saturday morning, I wrote a letter, making known I was available for revival. About one week later, I got an answer, inviting me to come for the whole month of April. So, I rode the Greyhound bus from Columbus to Winnipeg. I have been to Winnipeg many, many times now. My first trip however was a real walk of faith. .

It was my last night of the one month revival that Pastor Norman Murdock came with people from the Cree Indian Reserve at Koostatack (Fisher River) Manitoba. He invited me to come and preach to the Indians, little did I know this was the full-filling of something God had shown me years before. Through that humble beginning, God opened many doors; the North Country; our ministry to Cree, and Ojibway Indians started in Winnipeg.

Charles E. Pratt, Jr.

6.

From Milk to Meat

"I have fed you with milk and not with meat. For hither to ye were not able to bear it..."
Corinthians 3:2

Even so our faith will grow, step by step, day by day, month by month, and year by year, our faith grows. As we meet new challenges, we must continue to pray through for breakthrough, striving daily to do God's perfect will.

A baby doesn't come out of its mother's womb running the four forty relays. You have to crawl before you can walk, and walk before you can run. As it is in the natural, so is it in the Spirit. Faith takes time and greater faith takes even more time.

You start out taking baby steps. Here a little and there a little. God will start you out doing something small, that will progress into something large.

Whom shall he teach knowledge? and whom shall He make to understand doctrine? them that are weaned from the milk, and drawn from the breasts. For precept must be upon precept, precept upon precept; line upon line, line upon line; here a little, and there a little: For with stammering lips and another tongue will He speak to this people. Isaiah 28: 9, 10, 11

I remember being challenged to take a trip to Delaware, Ohio. It was the dead cold of winter. The snow seemed to be coming from all directions that evening. Common sense said, "Throw in the towel and say "Not tonight." but I heard the Lord saying "Go! Trust Me. I'll lead thee!" So we took off by faith. Somehow the snow storm blocked our view and we passed by the Delaware, Ohio exit. Pastor Jimmie Walton and I were so caught up talking about the goodness of the Lord, that we didn't realize we had passed Delaware. We looked up and the road sign read Mansfield, Ohio, seven miles. We had driven forty miles out of the way. By the time we would have turned around, it would be too late for service in Delaware.

"I know a church in Mansfield, that's having service tonight." Jimmie said. So, we went on to Faith Temple Church of God in Christ, Mansfield, Ohio, where L. G. Maddox was pastor. Little did I know how much God was in the plan. I didn't know what He was doing or what He would do.

The leading of the Lord is a wonderful and powerful thing. Often God leads us one step at a time. If He told us the complete plan, we probably wouldn't believe it. I preached in Mansfield that night and was invited back for a revival. I ended up moving to and working out of Mansfield with Dad Maddox for seven years. Through the Pastor and Ministry in Mansfield, countless doors were opened. It was all in God's plan and in His timing. It was a graduate course in *faith works*.

Charles E. Pratt, Jr.

7.

Faith Works through Love

It has been said, faith hope and love but the greatest of these is love.

"And now abideth faith, hope, and charity, these three; but the greatest of these is charity."

I Corinthians 13:13

The Greek for love is translated charity here. Charity suggests a love at work or our love in action. The love of Jesus Christ making good things happen in the midst of those we are among. So faith works through our acts of loving kindness one to another; hands that care, hands in prayer, and helpful hands that seek to share. I speak of faith at work through the administration of love. Our supplications, our good deeds, and our efforts to see the needs of others met. Faith goes to work in a Christian heart holding on to

God while helping others up. Through acts of kindness and deeds in mercy we manifest God's love in action. Love is the end result, our final answer to a lost and dying world. Fanny Crosby has said, "All the way my Savior leads me; what have I to ask beside? Can I doubt His tender mercy, who through love has been my guide?"

8.

When Faith Is Applied

"Now faith is the substance of things hoped for, the evidence of things not seen."

Heb. 11:1

Be an eye witness to the wonder working power of faith applied. Testify about the before and after of faith. Miracles, healing, blessings, and more will be realized daily when faith is applied.

Why not benefit out of your deficit; visualize success and venture, be a risk taker and take over, attack your lack and make the devil get back, stand on faith and defeat, defeat. "Reduce fear and worry, and get what you need and want by applying faith.

When you start to act upon faith rather than

just talk upon faith, good things begin to happen. You go from the problem to the promise, from the rite of affirmation of faith, to the right of application of faith. It's not so much what you say about faith but what you do about faith that counts.

Application speaks of the active putting on of a thing. We put on purpose, we set in motion a remedy and we demonstrate a principle. By application, we requisition faith; we effectively put our believing and trusting into action. We by application realize the relevancy of faith and how it connects for us in meeting all our needs.

I trust that the selections in the volume will cause you to stretch out on faith, the Bible says without faith it is impossible, hopeless, not feasible, utterly objectionable, to please or satisfy God. It is my desire for you that you take faith and make it work for you. May you come to the place where your faith moves, mountains.

9.

Application for Situation

"Not that I speak in respect of want: for I have learned, in whatsoever state I am, there with to be content."

Philippians 4:11

Life with its ups and downs can be in the best sense of the expression a real roller coaster ride. Paul our New Testament preacher, teacher, missionary, and apostle, experienced it all and he writes "who shall separate us from the love of Christ? Shall tribulation, or distress, or persecution, or famine, or nakedness, or peril, or sword? As it is written, "For thy sake we are killed all the day long; we are accounted as sheep for the slaughter. Nay in all these things we are more than conquerors through him that loved us. For I am persuaded, that neither death, nor life, nor angels, nor principalities, nor powers, nor things present, nor things to come, nor height, nor depth, nor any other creature, shall be able to separate us from the love of God which is in Christ Jesus our Lord."

Romans 8:35-39

Paul was a man who exercised faith application for every situation. The devil and his crew make no special exemptions for *deep people* or *holy men*; he keeps enough hell going to get the best of the best if he can. We are told, "If it were possible, he would deceive the very elect." Matt 24:24

So we need application for situation! We must make the practice of faith a daily habit in our rising up and lying down.

Wake up believing, lay down thanking and blessing his name for receiving. You can't afford to put your shield of faith down. The enemy doesn't stop shooting his fiery darts just because you've won a battle or two.

Finally, my brethren, be strong in the Lord, and in the power of his might. Put on (apply by faith) *the whole armour of God, that ye may be able to stand against the wiles of the devil. For we wrestle not against flesh and blood, but against principalities, against powers, against the rulers of the darkness of this world, against spiritual wickedness in high places. Wherefore take unto you the whole armour of God, that ye may be able to withstand in the evil day, and having done all to stand, stand therefore, having your loins girt about with truth, and having on the breastplate of righteousness; and your feet shod with the preparation of the gospel of peace; Above all, taking the shield of faith, wherewith ye shall be able to quench all the fiery darts of the wicked. And take the helmet of salvation, and the sword of the Spirit, which is the Word of God: Praying always with all prayer and supplication in the Spirit, and watching thereunto with all perseverance and supplication for all saints.*

Ephesians 6:10-18

Situation calls for the give and take of faiths application day after day. We never know who or what we're going to meet from one day to the next. Therefore we want to be sure that our faith is up to par. That our armour is in tack, and that we can overcome any attack of the enemy.

Above all taking the shield of faith! This of course speaks figuratively, not literally. There's no brass or metal shield that can stop the mental and spiritual warfare that seeks to depress us, destroy us, and completely defeat us.

The shield of faith is that application of faith built up through dedication and devotion, prayer and praise, Bible study and meditation. The Psalmist has said, in His law doeth he meditate day and night, and he shall be like a tree planted by the waters that bringeth forth his fruit in his season; his leaf also shall not wither, and whatsoever he doeth shall prosper.

Psalm 1:2, 3

Yes, you can be confident no matter what the situation. The word confidence actually means confide in God from the Latin root, 'confi- deo' meaning confide in God. I wrote these words in a song, titled *Put your trust in the Lord*, "When the weights of this world have got you down, when your going around with your head to the ground, put your trust in the Lord, put all your trust in the

Lord!"

Gospel singer Andréa Crouch says, "But in every situation, God gave blessed consolation, that my trials come to only make me strong, through it all."

"I've got confidence; we sing in our song service, the Lord is going to see me through no matter what the case may be, the Lord is going to fix it for me!"

More Than a Conqueror

Conquer the quirks and

Life's ups and downs

Quest the mountain top

Never to drown

Connect with a smile

Not with a frown.

Determine to live

With your feet off the ground

Inspire stability with

High thoughts of God

Walk by faith above earth and sod.

Realize no doubt, You're part of a plan.

Determine therefore to do

More than you can!

10.

THE WALK EXCEEDING THE TALK

Let us understand the difference between the talk of faith and the walk of faith. When I was in high school, we used a very to-the-point expression, "Talk is cheap!" In other words it was not enough to talk a good talk about something, and then not be able to walk the walk. Seeing a thing done exceeded an endless conversation about how great a runner, basket-baller, footballer, ping-ponger, singer, player, dancer, artist, or *brain* somebody was. We read these words out of God's Holy Word as they relate to the walk exceeding the talk, in reference to faith in God.

What doeth it profit, my brethren, though a man say he hath faith, and have not works? Can faith save him? If a brother or sister be naked, and destitute of daily food, and one of you say unto them, Depart in peace, be ye warmed and filled; and not withstanding ye give them not those things which are needful to the body; what doeth it profit? Even so faith, if it hath not works, is dead, being alone. Yea, a man may say, Thou hast faith, and I have works: shew me thy faith without thy works, and I will shew thee my faith by my works.

James 2:14-18

The teaching here reflects wonderfully on what I call activated faith, that's the faith that would rather walk than talk. 'Activated faith' actually does something tangible and profitable about all this believing. Activated faith joins believing with receiving. It's remunerative, useful and so beneficial. When you walk in faith you're going from the disadvantage of the talk alone, to all the advantages of the walk in tone. Yes, you can do what you say and go singing all along the way. The song says, "As I travel through this land singing as I go, pointing souls to Calvary through that crimson flow, many arrows pierce my soul from without, within, but my Lord leads me on, and through him I must win. Yes, *"We are more than conquerors through Christ."*

Romans 8:37

It's not about how much poetry, physiology, philosophy, principles, and even scripture you can quote, that constitutes a walk of faith. You can be a walking encyclopedia with a dead faith. Always theorizing, prognosticating, generalizing, and mythicizing as to what can and cannot be. *"I can do all things through Christ which strengtheneth me."* Philippians 4:13

So then, he strengthens you, not just so you can talk the talk, but far better, that you can walk the walk. It's not enough to talk about resource and all the power in the force of faith.

You have to take some walking steps, trusting that he is going to provide the power and vigor necessary to fully walk the walk. Believe without a doubt that he is toning your spiritual leg muscles, intensifying your determination to walk on. *"Yea though I walk through the valley of the shadow of death, I will fear no evil; for thou art with me, thy rod and thy staff they comfort me."* Psalm 23:4

Walking on, qualifies the believer not only to

take the test, but to easily pass the test! So walking faith walks on in spite of whatever you are going through. You never walk alone, you take his Word with you, and you take it at total face value. You are leaning, trusting, and always depending on the power of his everlasting arms.

You stand firm on the Excellency of his Holy Word. You walk your walk and stand your stand based on this original article that God cannot lie! *"God is not a man, that he should lie; neither the son of man, that he should repent: hath he said, and shall he not do it? Or hath he spoken, and shall he not make it good? Behold, I have received commandment to bless: and he hath blessed and I cannot reverse it.*

Numbers 23:19-20

Faith works, faith functions, the faith walk isn't phony, but a phenomenal fact, that when in tack, you will attack your lack. No need to doubt and go without; no need to make up elusive excuses for doing without. Walking the walk brings you to the basic reality of can do. I can do all things through Christ. Yes, you graduate from I can't to I can, from living in the negative to living in the positive, from being down in the dumps to coming out of the slumps. "I walk by faith and not by sight, in trusting depth with all my might, though storms bring boisterous gale and hail, my faith in Christ does ere assail, I shall not look on gravest trouble with doubt and fear and grumble I keep the faith with a heartfelt nod I walk by faith my eyes on God."

The 'From To' Of Faith

From the affirmation

Of faith,

To the application

Of faith

From the problem

To the promise

From the legal

To the regale

From the letter of the word

To the spirit of the letter

Let faith be applied

And never denied

'Faith Always Works'

Faith never gives up but looks up.

Will see you through

Makes dreams come true.

Sees through blinded eyes

Declares the empty hand full

An invincible tool

Faith develops abstracts into tangibles.

Offsets the negative

Sets off the positive

Climbs over adversity

Cultivates life's blessings

Reaches, teaches, and preaches.

Makes hopes into reality.

Explodes into miracles, **Faith always works!**

Keep Keeping On

Keep peddling, keep rowing, keep running.

Pitch for strike, swing for a homer,

Catch for an out.

Quitting is not part of the deal,

So stay cool, keep keeping it real.

Dare not the game to lose

Refuse to blow a fuse.

Stay in the competition

No time for remission.

Keep your mind for winning strong.

Push your body to play along.

Seek to keep your winning stride.

So hold your head in winning pride.

We Faithful

Characteristic are we faithful?

Intriguing courage we fulfill

Eagerly desirous of God's perfect will

Such particular behavior efficiency and skill

Exerting the faith, devoted in pace

We celebrate God's blessed grace.

Catechizing and always rising.

Victories are not surprising.

Qualified we take a stand.

Casting out the devil's plan

Advantages we give to God,

Leverage on the road we trod.

Charles E. Pratt, Jr.

11.

"High Praise Stirs High Faith"

"... And the wind ceased, and there was great calm, and he said unto them, "Why are ye so fearful? How is it that ye have no faith?

Mark 4: 39-40

Jesus had said to his disciples, "Let us pass over unto the other side." He wasn't talking about death and the other side of life, but simply to the opposite side of the sea. Jesus being Jesus knew full well that a tempest storm would arise in the midst of the sea, even as storms do rise in our own lives from time to time. This was a test in *Faith Maintenance* 101. I say if you expect to get an A in *Faith Maintenance* 101 you had better learn how to maintain your faith. There is no need for needless fear. Fear makes a total freak out of faith rendering it inoperative and inopportune. All to many of the saints are running around with their faith out of use and out of time, this ought not be , you need- ever ready faith.

When your faith is maintained your blessings cannot be contained. Let me give you some insider information on faith maintenance. High praise stirs high faith. Create or get in an atmosphere conducive to great praise. Find a full gospel church where they believe in hand-clapping, toe-tapping and tambourine-slapping, where ministry encourages and challenges you to lift your hands in the air and praise God like you just don't care. We are informed in scripture that God dwells in the very midst of our praises.

"But thou art holy, o thou that inhabits the praises of Israel"

Psalm 22:3

I have a very formative formula for generating high faith in folks. I say this, "Reach up in high praise, because high praise stirs high faith." "Praise him, praise him, praise him, because, because, because of the wonderful things He does."

When you learn to lift your hands in high praise

you can begin to pull down miracles in high faith. Faith unlocks the flood gates to divine supply and praise brings faith to its boiling point.

Praise is to faith, as oil is to an automobile, praise lubricates faith's engine, engineering a smooth activity of all the necessary parts.

Praise applies Holy oil to our trusting and believing and it loosens our hopes and dreams. Praise unfastens the bonds and fetters that the devil has sought to firmly fix on our situation. Praise your way through to victory!

"To appoint unto them that morn in Zion, to give unto them beauty for ashes, the oil of joy for mourning, the garment of praise for the spirit of heaviness; that they might be called trees of righteousness, the planting of the Lord, that he might be glorified." Isaiah 61: 3

We find great moves and manifestations of the Lord being kicked off or initiated by powerful praise. Throughout the precious pages of Holy Writ we find praise the preparatory pre-requisite for the move of God. When OLE Joshua *fit the battle of Jericho* it was high praise that penetrated the so called insurmountable walls of Jericho and brought them down flat. Yes, the walls came tumbling down, whatever the walls in your life faith will bring them down. Walls of fear, tension, test, insufficiency, sickness, pain, poverty, those 'High places' must come down. When faith is maintained your situation cannot remain the same! When OLE Gideon took the Midians with a minuscule army of only three hundred men, we find praise preceding the miracle victory.

It was praise at Pentecost that ushered in that Holy Ghost baptism. Therefore we must get on the good foot of high praise, always stirring up high faith. Because, faith in test, and faith in time; kills trouble all the time.

High praise works as a spiritual filter, for bringing us into the presence of God. I have said; first natural then spiritual. Your automobile has incorporated filtration in its system. The air filter, the gas filter and the water filter. All this filtering is there to keep the engine clean. Praise filters the filthy, the dirty, the unclean, and the nasty. It separates our mind, heart, and soul from that carnal garbage that seeks to hinder us. Praise removes the dirt and grime lifting us into the holy presence of God.

… Whatsoever things are true, whatsoever things are honest, whatsoever things are just, whatsoever things are pure, whatsoever things are lovely, whatsoever things are of good report; if there be any virtue, and if there be any praise, think on these things. Philippians 4-8

Growing Faith

My faith is growing

Day by day

My faith is growing

As I go on my way

My faith is growing

As I daily pray

My faith is growing

I believe what I say.

Giving Love

The timeless mark of giving love,

Is manifest through God above.

And what of the burdens we bare,

They grow out of love that we share.

Hope and faith and dreams serene,

And loving from the heart so keen,

Bespeaks those virtues rarely seen.

When love upon my heart display,

The light that makes all darkness day.

To know Christ Jesus is the Way.

Faithful in God's Word

Don't be tripped up or ripped up

Betwixt and between.

Don't be in a bout or in a doubt

Bewildered and demeaned.

Best to rest up on God's Holy Word.

Trust the preaching you have heard.

Keep the Faith and don't turn away,

Though storms of life may come your way,

Be lengthened and strengthened,

Believe and receive.

Be fruitful and faithful

To the Word of God take heed!

Why Not More Than

More than just a boast

of faith.

Why not make the most

of faith.

More than just a talk

of faith.

Why not make a walk

of faith.

More than just a read

of faith.

Why not take a lead

of faith.

More than just a seed

of faith.

Why not do a deed

of faith.

More than just a token

of faith.

Why not have a spoken

FAITH!

Faith Is All In All

Faith in God is all in all.

Faith stands up strong and tall.

Faith breaks down Satin's stubborn wall.

Faith empowers for the call.

Faith will never let you fall.

Faith stays right on top the ball.

Faith has a Godly kind of gall.

Faith puts you in business hall.

Faith will witness in the shopping mall.

Faith will take and make the devil stall.

A Faith Lift

When you're trampled with trouble and drift.

Let faith be your anchor and lift.

Up from conditions that torment and taunt

Life is brighter when faith starts to flaunt.

Parading about and casting out doubt.

Praising the lord and daring to shout.

So lift your voice in a sacred song.

Claiming, the victory all the day long.

Practice Faith

Learn to practice faith.

   Smile and don't frown.

Hold your head up high, and not always down.

The eyes of faith blot out the negative

Because faith looks up, and only sees the positive.

Faith will furnish ascending vision

A powerful, positive, point-blank decision.

To see farther than darkest despair and gloom

Visualizing, recognizing

    there's plenty, of room

For improvement in our life style at present,

Faith looks beyond dark days unpleasant.

Sees them as stepping stones for a brighter tomorrow

Faith looks up and away from present sorrow.

Faith sees love, joy, and blissful peace,

    Through the practice of faith

Life's blessings increase!

The Devil Comes

When Jesus comes with an open arm,

The devil comes to cause alarm.

When Jesus comes with abundant life,

The devil comes to stir up strife.

When Jesus comes to save and heal,

The devil comes to kill and steal.

When Jesus comes to right the wrong,

The devil comes to break the strong.

When Jesus comes to see you through,

The devil comes to bother you.

Heaven's Blessings

Miracles, healings, blessings and more

Realize them daily through Faith's
open door.

Know no doubt He'll never leave us.

When faith is applied in Christ Jesus.

There is so much power in that name.

When faith is applied there is no
shame.

Rise above being mad and sad,

Because what you want can sure be
had.

When your wants have been delayed,

Apply your faith when you have
Prayed.

Take some steps, do some pressing.

Open up for heaven's blessing.

The Father wants to fill your cup.

Apply your faith and lift it up!

Faith Builds

Faith is central and essential

Turning dreams into realities.

Faith takes a can't making it a can

I can do all things through Christ.

Faith makes the unattainable

Attainable

It builds the unbuildable

It goes for the goal

It finds the gold

Faith is a process ending in success.

It keeps on believing.

To the point of receiving

It goes beyond trying

To the place of applying

It inherits the promises

By the power of the Promiser.

It overcomes great instability

And produces true ability.

I Shan't Recant

As for me I shan't recant

The Gospel Message so blatant

To love, forgive and give,

To follow Christ on how to live.

To walk upright and do what's good,

To treat my neighbors as I should,

To blend with friends and seek to lend

A helping hand whenever I can.

And live for Christ until the end.

It's a New Day

Stop living in the squalor of yesterday

Realize with each new day

There's a new chance

To turn defeat into advance,

To turn disappointment into enjoyment

To turn gloom into bloom,

To turn from looking down

Into looking up,

> *Behold it's a New Day!*

Discover the Counterfeiter

Discover the counterfeiter where he be,

Speaking primarily for a colossal fee.

Steering the helm, piloting the plane,

Speaking things senselessly and insane.

Walking on eggshells, tipping on high toes,

Clad in religious super sainted clothes,

Circumventing our true Gospel Message,

Disloyal to every sacred passage.

Clandestine in pursuit to make a hit,

Out to outwit the page of Holy Writ.

Discover the counterfeiter where he be

My Faith

My faith stands faithful in spite of the problem

Patiently and persistently waiting on the promise

When dark clouds gather and folks act so rude

All gloomy and sullen as the world would elude

My faith comes around in a good spirited mood

I'm confiding in Christ so I shall not brood

My faith sees hope on the down trodden slope

I'm residing in Christ so I shall not mope

My faith takes the victory, the devil is put out

I'm striding in Christ so I shall not doubt

Hold On and Let Go

Put believing and trusting in gear

Hold on to faith let go of fear

If you use what you have

You can have what you want

Good things start to happen

When faith starts to flaunt

Jump on that old devil

And let him know better

Refuse to be, tormented and fettered

Stand on faith's ground

And in Jesus be found

Dare to declare your own territory

And with faith in Jesus give him glory

12.

Success and Blessings

"Looking unto Jesus the author finisher of our faith who for the joy that was set before him endured the cross, despising the shame, and is set down at the right hand of the throne of God"

Hebrew 12,2

Nothing works more wonderfully than faith, setting into motion success and blessings in life. Faith however, does not work in voluntarily. The working of faith is not by chance but rather in taking chance. Faith looks up when everything seems down, allowing God control of the situation. Faith makes a calculated decision to trust in God.

In the very midst of the immovable mountain or the seeming immutable snare, faith looks to Him. The praise, the prayer, the worship, which faith generates, begets incredible blessings where there were none, springs in the dessert, bountiful supplies, circumstances suddenly changed, and boom the flood gates are opened! Hallelujah!

"The earth is the Lord's and the fullness thereof; The world, and they that dwell therein for he hath founded it upon the seas, and established it upon the floods. Who shall ascend into the hill of the Lord? Or who shall stand in his Holy place?

He that hath clean hands, and a pure heart; who hath not lifted up his soul unto vanity, nor sworn deceitfully. He shall receive the blessings from the Lord, and righteousness from the God of his salvation. This is the generation of them that seek him, that seek thy face,
Psalm 24, 1-6

13.

Speaking Of Seeking

Speaking of seeking, the hymnologist has a powerful discourse, "Prayer is the key to heaven but faith unlocks the door" How potent and influential this faith at work in opening doors. Whenever we are found seeking the Lord, faith is definitely working.

In the midst of seeking God, mere theory becomes clear reality. Here it is, *"Seek and ye shall find, knock and the door shall be opened.*

Matthew 7,7

Whenever faith starts a-knocking, the unseen becomes clearly seen. Dark clouds dissipate and sunshine disposes darkness. Working faith puts a spell check on the troublesome word reality. You can then begin to spell (R E A L I T Y) in the concrete materialistic terms of (R E A L T Y). As you work your faith you arrive at your dream. You go from beholding to actually holding, from the abstract to the fact. Faith works until you literally attain and gain possession. Faith works toward occupation of the thing you're believing God for.

When you invest your faith in God, you will realize prosperity, spelled property. You can have the new, the better, and the very best. the house, the car, the boat, the business, the faith, the working faith, undoes the unbelief, producing an unfettered expectancy that, *"I can do all things through Christ which strengtheneth me."*

Philippians 4, 13

Faith works with insistence and demanding persistence. It doesn't give up but looks up. It always works.

Faith Works

Faith Works

Faith works in spite of all life's

greatest fears

Faith works regardless of your

worries and tears

Faith works when dark clouds

obscure the view

Faith works effectively to

see you through

Faith works when Satan comes

to hinder you

Faith works when you don't know

what to do

Faith works to give your spirit depth

Faith works to put pep into your step

Faith works though come what

    daily may

Faith works to lead you all

    along the way

Charles E. Pratt, Jr.

When Faith Is Applied

When faith is applied,

      the problems step aside.

When faith is applied,

      the demons run and hide.

When faith is applied,

      the peace of God abide.

When faith is applied,

      Gods grace is on your side.

When faith is applied,

      the blessing's in the tide.

When faith is applied,

      the miracles coincide.

When faith is applied,

      the Holy Ghost will guide.

When faith is applied,

        you'll pick up on your stride.

When faith is applied,

        you'll have sense of pride.

When faith is applied,

        you will be fortified.

When faith is applied,

        Ole Satan cannot ride.

Charles E. Pratt, Jr.

Faith Over All

Faith over fear

Faith over foolishness

and

Faith over fable

Faith over fault

and

Faith over fakery

Faith over fiction

and

Faith over flop

Faith over fad

and

Faith over fabricating

Faith over fussing

and

Faith over feuding

Faith over fending

`and

Faith over falsehood

Faith over fib

and

Faith over flattery

Faith over fury

and

Faith over fist

Faith over flight

and

Faith over fainting

Faith over failing.

Charles E. Pratt, Jr.

14.

Faith and Fruit

"He was hungry and seeing from afar a fig tree having leaves, He went to see if perhaps He would find something on it when he came to it. He found nothing but leaves, for it was not the season for figs, In response, *Jesus said to it, "Let no one eat fruit from you ever again." And His disciples heard it.*

Mark 11; 13-14

"Now in the morning, as they passed by they saw the fig tree dried up from the roots, and Peter remembering said to Him Rabbi, look! The fig tree which you cursed has withered away. So Jesus answered and said to them, "Have faith in God."

"For assuredly, I say to you whoever says to this mountain, be removed and be cast into the sea, and does not doubt in his heart, but believes that those things He says will be done he will have whatever He says."

"Therefore I say to you whatever things you ask when you pray, believe that you receive them, and you will have them." Mark 11: 20-22

As we live our life based on the Bible, blessings will overtake us. The Bible is the backer, the banker, the broker, and the booker, for every blessing and promise that belongs to us.

15.

The Attitude of Faith

Faith in test and faith in time kills trouble all the time. The attitude of faith will produce within you the altitude for flying high in the face of a storm.

Up from the pit and into the palace. Out of the ditch and on to the highway of success. Up from the dark damp dingy basement where mold and mildew kill to a bright and beautiful new living room; the place, full of Jesus Christ light.

With the attitude of faith, you rejoice because the light has come into your world. You now fly high. No more negative cackling with the barn yard chickens, but your flying high over mountain tops with eagles. Scripture tells you to go ahead, *"Mount up on wings as eagles, run and not be weary, walk and not faint."*

Isaiah 40:31

For every negative action, there is an equal and opposite 'Faith' reaction. Faith is your other option. This was the lesson our Lord taught when He cursed the unfruitful fig tree. The students wanted to know, how the tree had withered away over night. Jesus does not give them an advanced scientific explanation. He simply says, "Have faith in God." We are empowered by faith in God to curse the negativity from day to day. Talk to the bad situation and tell it to get stepping. React with a positive faith reaction. When my oldest granddaughter was small, she would say, "I can't want it Papa." Exercise faith for what you want.

16.

Existence and Persistence

I found out full well that day after day existence calls for day after day persistence. You have to hold the line, keep pushing, keep pressing. Yes, working faith, keeps keeping on. It doesn't quit. It keeps trusting, believing, and therefore keeps receiving.

After while you get the <u>will</u> to know that God will. You learn that God can't lie; He said what He meant and meant what He said. You arrive at this fundamental place– God said it, I believe it and that settles it!!! The fact of Bible-believing faith is that faith is unwavering. You can know that you know that you know.

James 1; 6

"But let him ask in faith nothing wavering. For he that wavereth is like a wave of the sea driven with the wind and tossed."

You learn not to be tossed. You learn to stand your ground.. *"My hope is built on nothing less, than Jesus Christ and righteousness."*

17.

Working Faith

My faith, my working faith, my *Holy Bible Believing Faith*, is not a rite or ritual. It's not a religious mind over matter, half-baked superstitious humdrum thing. No, it is not a <u>rite</u>, but a <u>right</u>. Yes, a right to every promise in that book called the Bible. "The B I B L E, yes that's the book for me. I stand alone on the Word of God, the B I B L E." I learned that song in Sunday school and they would combine another song with it. "Every promise in the Book is mine, every chapter every verse, every line. I'm standing on the promises divine, cause every promise in the Book is mine."

I will never forget my first encounter with a real faith miracle. It was my tenth grade year in high school I had started attending the New

Revival Center, "Christ Cathedral" in Columbus, Ohio. They had bought the former *Eastern Theater* building, where as a child, we would go on Saturdays and see cartoons; Walt Disney's, and all those monster movies; *King Kong, It Came from Beneath the Sea , Space Creatures,* Science Fiction, and Jerry Lewis comedies, etc, and etc.

The Pastor of the Church testified that God told him to leave Wellston, Ohio and go to Columbus, Ohio. Drive east on Main St. and open up a church in the cinema. The pastor's name was Paul Andrew Christian, and the secretary's name was Marvin Blessing. I quickly got to know Paul Christian and began working around the building and helping the pastor in any way needed.

On one particular day, I arrived at the pastor's residence, which happened to be right across the street from the church. He was sitting on the porch, smiling in the sunshine. "I would offer you lunch," he said, "But , we don't have any food in the house."

"No food," I said, "What are you going to do?"

"I was just getting ready to 'Pray,' when you walked up. Give me a minute." The man raised his hands in the air, raised his voice in a simple prayer. It went something like this: "Thank you in advance for answering my prayer Dear Lord." We have no food right now, and I need you to supply." He talked to God in that prayer just as though he was talking to a billionaire friend.

"Lord, he prayed, I'd like some fresh fruit, and vegetables, some big apples, peaches, and pears, some blueberries, and raspberries, some of those juicy grapes, some nice bananas, collard greens, and cabbage, potatoes, and big watermelons, I want some milk and honey, I would like some meat, some T-bone steaks, pork chops, some chickens." "Thank you, Lord, for meeting my needs. Amen! Hallelujah, Hallelujah, and Hallelujah!"

No sooner than the man had said Amen, I heard the loud screech of tires on the street, then, "Ca-bang!" Suddenly two men stood at the bottom of that porch holding boxes. "Can you use any of these fruits or vegetables?"   "We just spilled our load in the street over there and we're not allowed to put it back on the truck."

"Thank you," said the pastor.   "Put it right here."

Every thing he asked for in the way of fruit and vegetables was suddenly there on the porch in front of us.   Then the next-door neighbor came over. "We're just returning from my father's farm in the country, and thought you'd like some fresh milk and honey." They gave him a giant tin of honey, Five gallons and a Five gallon cylinder full of fresh milk.

Then, here comes Brother Marvin Blessing, from Bexley, Ohio, with a dozen bags of meat from the *Big Bear Super Market.*   "We felt impressed to bring you some meat." He said.

A good thirty minutes hadn't gone by, and everything the pastor asked for was at his feet. Every thing he asked in prayer was there!

That evening various church members brought

can goods. Food poured in so much so, that baskets were made and the excess food was promptly being given away. Yes faith works and Jesus never fails!

We resonate by reflecting on faith. Faith makes for that determination to succeed, and so you succeed when that next step is followed by another and another, and another, etc, etc., and etc. You keep pressing. Yes press for success! Never give up. Don't stop believing. Do something about your doubt. In football terms; Faith takes first and ten, turning it into first and goal, to go. It pushes forward, it makes the score. It wins. We are told that Jesus is author and finisher of our faith.   He guarantees that you finish in the winning. You win when you work. *"Work at First, Win at Last."*

For every negative action, there's an equal and opposite 'Positive' reaction. The pastor's prayer was an attack on his lack, and it worked a miracle wonder.

Charles E. Pratt, Jr.

18.

Ever Ready Faith

Do you have *ever ready faith* or *never ready faith*? Ever ready faith speaks in terms of my stated maximum. "When your faith is maintained, your blessings cannot be contained." Ever ready faith is what it is, because, we're persistent in prayer, praise, Bible study, and church attendance. Your close relationship with the Lord, boosters -your faith. The afore mentioned things, bring faith to an ever ready boiling point. Just like in sports, you have to prepare for the contest, workout, practice, spend-time -on- the court, or in the field. You have got to get ready! Never ready faith– doesn't do anything in preparation for the battle, so get ready and be ready we are told *the battle is not to the swift or the strong, but to those who stay in there.*

Ecclesiastics 9; 11

So stay on the battlefield. Keep keeping on!

The 13th chapter of Numbers tells the remarkable story of God's people spying out the land. They came back with opposite attitudes: One of fear, the other of faith. Fear saw the giants, the sons of Anak, which come of the giants, and we were in our own sight as grasshoppers. Yes, grasshoppers, with the face of fear, but victorious, over comers, winners, with the face of faith.

"..And Caleb stilled the people before Moses, and said let us go up at once and possess it; for we are well able to overcome it." Numbers 13; 30

Do you walk with the face of fear or do you walk with the face of faith? Fear, never works, but faith **always** works.

19.

The Face of Faith

When you look into the face of faith, you will soon realize that faith isn't scared, backward, and weak.. The face of faith is bold, determined, and resolute. The ole song says, "I am determined to hold out to the end. Jesus is with me on Him I can depend." So, why not look forward and dare to pursue your pursuits. The face of faith is firm. Faith has a purpose, so faith takes a position. Its posture is fixed toward believing the Word of God. The face of faith will always tend to the concept that God can't lie. *"God is not a man that He should lie; neither the son of man, that He should repent; hath He said, and shall He not do it? or hath He spoken, and shall He not make it good?"* Numbers 23; 19

You can let faith work to replace the fear and

negativity on your face. You need "A faith lift," for "A face lift." Refuse to lose! Refuse to go through life with a scowl or a frown on your face. Remember, faith looks up, and not down. Try getting an expression of faith, good expectation, rather than bad exasperation. "Put on a happy face." Say, "I believe God!" Faith in God's promises and goodness will turn your sad face– happy. Psalms, says, "I was glad when they said unto me; let us go into the house of the Lord." "He has made me glad." "I will rejoice!" In spite of irregularities of life the difficulty, the bad people, and bad circumstances you face, God has prepared for you a happy face.

God gave Ezekiel a faith to face all those rebellious faces. Ezekiel 8; 8 (Eight being the number of new beginnings), we read; *"Behold, I have made your face strong against their faces, and thy forehead strong against their forehead."*

Vs. 9) says; *"As an adamant harder than flint, have I made thy forehead: Fear them not, neither be dismayed at their looks, though they be a rebellious house."*

You need not be scared out of your wits, intimidated and terrorized, realize faith doesn't frighten but faith enlightens.

"For God, who commanded the light to shine out of darkness, hath shined in our hearts to give the light of the knowledge of the glory of God in the face of Jesus Christ." II Corinthians 4; 6

The eye of faith blots out the negative —

Faith looks in with introspection, and then faith looks out with expectation!

Its meditation and prayer, then working in high hope. Giving the Lord my time, talent, and treasure. Walking in His light is my greatest pleasure. Living for a plan, a purpose, and a place; Standing on the Lord's side, knowing His grace. God has a purpose for me, a special place for me to be. Prime time is in my reserve, for all the blessings I deserve, in God's plan, in God's purpose, and in God's place. *"For therein is the righteousness of God revealed, from faith to faith, as it is written"; "The just shall live by faith."* Hebrews 10; 38

"The just shall live by faith." Six short words, but within those six words, three of the most powerful of all human conceptions: That of **justice**, that of **life**, and that of **faith**. I believe the most powerful and potent of the three; That of faith, because faith transcends justice and life. The only true justice comes from God alone, and life itself is contingent upon God alone. Then faith alone brings one into justice and life with God everlasting.

We read in Hebrews 11; 6 *"But without faith it is impossible to please Him: for he that cometh to God must believe that He is..."* Without faith it is (Impossi -bible) I like to spell it like this. I like to say without the <u>Bible,</u> you can't please God. Now that is living by faith. Let faith be strong, when things go wrong!

I may not know for sure what the future holds, but I know for sure, who holds the future. Faith holds to a positive hope in God. So then living by faith is living on the guarantee of God's Word.

Living on the Bible, standing daily on the validity of His precious promises, knowing deep down inside, that all is well, Yes indeed "It's well with my soul."

Faith reinforces the **'I will'** over the 'I won't' or the 'I can't.'

Scripture tells us in no uncertain terms, "I can do all things through Christ, who strengthens me!"

Philippians 4, 13

Faith enforces the -will to do, to go, and therefore to get. Faith paints a picture of success. Unbelief paints a picture of darkness, of doom, and gloom.

The 'Faith Lift,' gives you the 'Face Lift' that takes you from the dance of anger to the dance of joy, from being a *rage-a-holic*, to becoming a *church-a-holic*.

Faith isn't a scientific breakthrough, but faith can make for the scientific breakthrough. Faith resolves to keep believing and moving ever forward.

It's the pray through for a breakthrough. No faith is not in happenstance, but faith is in taking a chance.

Emmanuel -God with us! Jesus said, *"For lo I am with you always, even unto the end of the world."* Matthew 28; 20

Yes, God for you, God in you, and God with you. *"If God be for you, who can be against you."* Romans 8; 31

He's more than the world against you, so my faith is often a portion distortion. A tiny little acorn, makes the big oak tree, and a tiny little mustard seed moves a giant mountain. Little is much when God is in it.

Charles E. Pratt, Jr.

20.

From Dependence to Transcendence

Faith steps into the unknown in order to truly know. Often overwhelmed with doubts and fears, faith dares to trust in God. Faith keeps stepping. *"It presses toward the mark, for the prize of the high calling of God in Christ Jesus."*

Philippians 3; 14

So then faith not only deepens, it also transcends. It takes another step. It goes another mile. Faith moves forward. *"And whosoever shall compel thee to go a mile, go with him twain."*

Matthew 5; 41

By faith, we transcend the trouble. We find this transcending faith throughout the Bible; presenting us with many a teaching lesson.

For whatsoever things were written afore time, were written for our learning, that we through patience and comfort of the scriptures

might have hope." Romans 15; 4

For everything written in the past was written to teach us, so that with the encouraging element of the Tamakh we might patiently hold on to our hope. Romans 15; 4 Jewish NT

The woman with the issue of blood, pushed forward, in order to just touch the hem of His garment. Matthew 9, 20 –22

Blind Bartimaeus, cried out in the midst of the crowd, *"Jesus have mercy on me."* Here again, faith is pushing, pressing, and pulling toward the mark. Yes faith keeps stepping up to the plate. It determines to hit a home run, and so it does. Matthew 20; 29-34

Then again, faith sometimes will remove the roof. The two friends took the invalid crippled man to Jesus. In order to get to Jesus, , they carried the bed-ridden man to the house top, tore a hole in the roof, and lowered the man to Jesus. Matthew 9; 2-8

In short, my faith is based on the subject matter of the Bible, there is a learning in all those precious Bible stories. *Daniel in the lion's den, David and Goliath, The three Hebrew boys in the fiery furnace* etc... in Bible history and background. It will ground you. It's the best education and instruction in life. No wonder Jesus quoted so often from Scripture. Then He says; Behold I come in the volume of the Book, Hebrews 10; 7

It is ease to the body, and total well-being to the whole man.

Charles E. Pratt, Jr.

21.

Don't Stop, Don't Quit

The message is simple, yet so profound. I remember traveling on the PA Turnpike, Judy and I were headed for Youngstown, Ohio. We were in one of those mighty winter snow blizzards, I wanted to stop. I would have quickly pulled over, but that was not an option. Mile after mile, things were getting worse. So often are the situations and storms in our lives, spiritual, physical, and financial. I could hear the Holy Ghost say, "Go another mile." Finally I could see the flicker of dim lights at a little motel, but the Lord seemed to still be saying, go another mile. In my desperation, I pulled into that motel because this was it I couldn't go any further. I named that place: 'Flea Bit– Rat Motel', @ $27.50 a night. We barely managed to stay warm and sleep that night.

We were glad to get out of there the next day.

The blizzard was over. We got on the road, went one mile up the hill and found every 4 and 5 star motel, we could think of, in that place. We just needed to *'Go another mile'*

22.

Effectual Prayer

"The effectual fervent Prayer of a righteous man availeth much." James 5; 16

Where we are limited, God is limitless. When we have gone as far as we can go, and done as much as we can do, some would say when we've reached the end of our rope, take hope, and just believe. God can and God

is, yes, *"He is a very present help in the time of trouble."* Psalm 46; 1

Let faith take effect, dare to do some praying. Know no doubt, that prayer works.

Prospect: That means expectation and anticipation, look forward for the reward. Thank God in advance for your advancement. It's going to happen, because; *"All things work together for the good to those who are the called according to His purpose."* Romans 8;28

Yes prospect– go for the gold.   It's yours already.

One more word;

Expect– Oral Roberts said it years ago. *"Expect a Miracle."* Expect by definition, to look forward to regard as going to happen, anticipate the occurrence of or coming off.

Faith is a can do, can be, will be. I can be wise, I can be well, I can be wealthy.

Let me say this, if you dare to work your faith, your faith will work for you.

God wants to get your attention, so that He can establish His very intention for your coming in and going out.

The devil, the enemy, the situation, comes to suggest that you can't do anything. He tries to give you a negative opinion. He seeks to mess with your mind, telling you, *"Things aren't going to be better, but only worse." "God does not hear you"* and *"The Bible isn't true,"* and *"There's not a thing you or anybody else can do about it. So give up– quit, throw in the towel, admit defeat,"* but, Scripture tells us, *"As a man thinketh in his heart, so is he."* Proverbs 23; 7

Let us therefore think in faith, believing in God's promises. Just say, 'Yes,' to His Word, to His will, and to His way.

Charles E. Pratt, Jr.

23.

Turn Aside

Faith is not stupidity, and stupidity is not faith. Stupidity implies slow-wittedness and the lack of normal intelligence. I have often said that the only difference between faith and stupidity is that God has spoken. When God speaks, that which is naturally dumb and stupid, becomes faith. Therefore, faith is that God has spoken. We do not understand the mind of God, so we submit, we quit and just say, 'Yes Lord. *"For my thoughts are not your thoughts. Neither are your ways my ways, saith the Lord. For as the heavens are higher than your ways, and my thoughts than your thoughts."*

Isaiah 55; 8-9

We are finite, and God Almighty is infinite. To exercise faith, we need to know what God is calling us to do. I have said, "Faith is knowing what God has called you to do and going out and doing it." Faith turns aside to do the will and purpose of God in ones life, Yes, you go for it.

"And Moses said, I will now turn aside, and see this great sight, why the bush is not burnt." And when the Lord saw that he turned aside to seek, God called unto him out of the midst of the bush, and said, "Moses, Moses," and he said, "Here am I." Exodus 3; 3-4

24.

What Faith Isn't

Faith is not something fictitious, or imaginary. It's not mythology or theology. Absolute Bible believing faith, Christian faith, pure faith, this faith that I preach and teach, is completely and totally contingent on God, on the Bible, on His Holy Word.

The song says, "I believe God, I believe God, ask what you will and it shall be done. Trust and obey. Believe Him, and say, I believe, I believe God."

It's not scientific, it's not mind over matter. No, faith is not a mind game. It's not something special we say, or a game we play. Faith in God and faith in His Word isn't a psych job.

Faith is not driving your car to the banks of the river, praying for the waters to part, when there's a bridge one mile down the road. Nor, is it sitting in your easy chair praying for God to translate you to a distance city, when a plane is leaving in one hour. When troubles and trails would cause you to scare, take hold of faith and handle with care.

25.

Our Bible

The Bible is the manufacture's manual for any and all things pertaining to mankind on the planet, in this present world and the world to come. It is an inspired revelation from beginning to end and reveals the beginning and the end. It is the answer to the greatest question of life, telling us who we are, why we are here, and where we are going. It gives us the keys to the kingdom, for life here and now and everlasting. It is the power of God unto abundant life and salvation. It is the source and resource for strengthening body, mind, and soul. It is God's will and testament to all men in all ages, regardless of race, creed, or gender. This will and testament is signed in Christ's own blood. It reveals God's plan, purpose, and place for man to apply his time, talent, and treasure. It is a book above books for within its sacred pages we behold the mind of God, the state of man, the way of life and the gate of heaven.

It is the believers blessing and the unbelievers stressing.

It is the believers building up and the unbelievers going down.

It is hope for the hopeless, joy for the joyless, and love for the loveless.

Study it to be stable, trust it to be strong, practice it to be upright, keep it to be clean. It contains light to guide you, food to feed you, and faith to carry you. It is the traveler's map, the pilgrim's staff, the pilot's compass, the soldier's sword and the Christian's charter.

Jesus Christ is its major subject, our good is its greatest design, and God in his glory is its CLIMAX! It should direct your heart, guide your feet, and rule your mind. Study it daily, prayerfully, carefully, searchingly, slowly, and continually. Study it until it becomes a part of you. It is healing, health, prosperity, and a mine of wealth.

The Bible is a can do, will to, source for success.

The Bible is not mind over matter but a matter of

fact.

The Bible is history and it's His story.

The Bible is a moving love story; it reveals Gods love for humanity.

The Old Testament is the New Testament concealed and the New Testament is the Old Testament revealed.

The Old Testament is the New Testament patent.

The New Testament is the Old Testament latent.

The Bible is a timeless message that's always on time.

The Bible is the world's best selling book.

The Bible has been translated into more languages than any other book.

It is a totally unique book given by God to man and in it God communicates to man.

The Bible contains 1,100 chapters in 66 books by many authors, spanning 1,600 years.

The Bible is not speculation but revelation.

The wisdom of the Bible pre dates everything and transcends all things.

The Bible instructs us in living the life, learning in life, and in everlasting life.

From cashmere to mere cash the Bible tells you how to cash in on God's blessings.

The Bible is not just inspiring but it is inspired by God.

The Bible is totally reliable and totally relevant.

Man would not have written the Bible if he could and could not have wrote the Bible if he would.

Never a more wonderful book.

Never a more important book, has ever been produced!

The first words in the Bible say; "In the beginning God." The Bible traces creation of the universe to a personal God. The Bible tells us man is unique and special made in the image of God.

The Bible affirms that man has a moral responsibility and reveals God's plan for man.

26.

Understanding the Bible

"Study to shew thyself approved unto God, a workman that needed not to be ashamed, rightly dividing the word of truth." II Timothy 2, 15

Where do we begin and where do we end? Bible study or what I like to call Deeper Life Study, isn't the work of an hour or two, it is the outworking of a lifetime. It requires the same type of diligent care that a gardener puts into cultivating, an angler puts into fishing, or a homemaker into the home.

We should always approach Bible studies prayerfully and carefully, with an open mind and an open heart, knowing that the knowledge within its pages is divine. God has spoken! There's a learning to be had.

"God who at sundry times and in diverse manners spake in times past unto the fathers by

the prophets hath in these last days spoken unto us by his son..." Hebrews 1, 1-2

Our attitude toward understanding what God has said, should be a principled and focused process in comprehension as well as composition. We need to know what God has said and then know how to apply it in our day to day living. The Word of God is an integral part of who we are and what we will be. As children of the Most High God, we have a relation to the Word, and as we seek understanding into deeper life we grow with a revelation of the Word,

"Thy word have I hid in mine heart, that I might not sin against thee." Psalm 119, 11

27.

On the Money

Faith is a sure power tool that works on the money too. I trust you will be careful as well as prayerful, when it comes to having the money you need for living and being who God has called you to be.

From the ranks of the rich to the ranks of the poor, we wrestle over money. Money, money, money, money is our medium of exchange, and measure of value.

Money could very well be the most paradoxical piece of paper on earth. Money seems to do and be everything, It buys love, pays for hate, purchases peace and pays for war!

No wonder the wise man said, *"Money*

answereth all things" Ecclesiastes 10: 19 and we are instructed in scripture the much quoted *"For the love of money is the root of all evil."*

I Timothy 6: 10

"Beloved, when I gave all diligence to write unto you, and exhort you that ye should earnestly contend for the faith which was once delivered unto the saints" Jude 3. Contend for the faith, not pretend for the faith!

To pretend is to claim or profess falsely to make believe.   We must not be pretenders, but contenders.   Contend– strive after, fight for, compete, hold to the fact, assert yourself, and continue to believe.

"When your faith is maintained, your blessings cannot be contained"   When you work your faith; your

Faith will work for you.   I've heard many mainliners preach faith for salvation, faith for the Holy Ghost, faith for healing, but when it comes to money, they don't believe.   The   buck   stops here.

I am a witness that faith has worked in every area of my life. The buck begins with faith in God in His Holy Word, knowing that He said what He meant, and He meant what He said.

God meant for you to exercise faith and believe for money miracles in your life. For the Christian believer, money miracles are the result of faith at work, or better said, faith that works.

Some would say, No! You're just lucky, you lucked out. I would like you to consider the total difference between luck and faith. Luck speaks of happenstance. Luck is inconsistent; some would say it's the unseen force that seems to operate for good in ones life, shaping events and opportunities; Luck-good fortune and success, luck finding work, luck finding money. Thank God, we of the *household of faith*, are not dependent on this unseen force that the world calls *luck*.

Faith on the other hand, speaks of trusting

and relying on God; Standing on God's Word, taking the Scriptures at face value. Faith is consistent, Faith works through an insistence in God and the assistance of God.

Faith is an optimist; it looks to the favorable side of life. It believes without question in the favor of God.

Faith believes in the overall predominance of good over evil, blessings over curses; the power of God to change things for the better.

The optimist says, I believe God, and faith works. While the poor pessimist is afraid that faith could very well work and God is a rewarder of them who diligently seek Him.

So, the pessimist lacks faith and is totally void of hope. He looks for negative things to happen. His out look on live is sullen and gloomy. He refuses to believe God.

I like to see working faith as enlisting a powerful positive charge into your very atmosphere. Yes faith blots out the negative energy all around you, charging the air with a positive flow.

Working faith, it has been called, *"The Power of Positive Thinking" "Possibility Thinking,"* that jolt of faith will get you moving in the right direction, and start things going for good. *It's "The-I- can do!" "The-My God Is," "The Name It and Claim It," "The-Speak It Into Existence," "The Call It Done"* Ext. Ext.

Yes that positive charge of faith nullifies the negative charge of doubt and unbelief, exploding into miracles and blessings for your life.

Charles E. Pratt, Jr.

28.

The Miracle of the Money

And when they were come to Capernaum, they that received tribute money, (The Jewish Temple Tax), came to Peter, and said, "Doeth not your Master pay tribute? He saith, Yes. And when he was come into the house, Jesus prevented him, saying, What thinkest thou, Simon? of whom do kings of the earth take custom or tribute? of their own children, or strangers? Peter saith unto Him, Of strangers. Jesus saith unto him, Then are the children free. Notwithstanding, lest we should offend them, go thou to the sea, and cast an hook, and take up the fish that first cometh up; and when thou hast opened his mouth, thou shalt find a piece of money: that take, and give unto them for me and thee."

St Matthew 17; 24– 27

This has been called the *Miracle of the Money.* Jesus says, "Go fishing," throw out a line, take the first fish you catch, open it's mouth, and you will find a gold piece. Yes, by faith, we can find the money that we need.

Fishing in the regular sense is about catching or perhaps not catching fish. Fish are caught indirectly. There's a sort of cunning required, an art applied. In this particular situation, Jesus sends the fishermen on a fishing trip.

In order to provide the payment, for the Temple

tax, Jesus waves the everyday normal prerogative and by miracle means, the *Lord of the Sea* goes to the sea. Peter is told to do his thing. Apply his trade, not with the everyday net, but with hook-and-line. What a wonderful way to make the miracle more striking. Jesus knew where the fish were and that the fish had gold in his mouth. Jesus can draw the fish from out of the deep, and cause him to take a hook, in order to put money in your hand.

It is not uncommon for fish to swallow shinny objects. Cod fish have been found with watches in their stomachs, still running. The wonder is that The God of the sea commands a fish in the sea to find Peter's hook and show him the money.

Faith and obedience to Jesus, has the power to create miracles and blessings. Yes we can bring into being the money we need to sustain us. Out of nothing, something. From gross darkness, to light, from, negativity to positively., from deep despair to high hope, and from poverty to prosperity, from rags to riches. No fairy tale, no farce, but a fact of faith, a work at work, through Jesus.

Jesus was preparing us to walk in faith and believe in money miracles. He was demonstrating right in

the middle of this need to pay a bill, ***miracle money.*** He wants you to know that He is your provider, your shepherd, and source. So do not despair in the midst of your trouble, but rather **trust!** **"Go fishing,"** and find a gold piece! *"Jesus Christ the same yesterday, today, and forever"* Hebrews 13; 8

"Perfecto" Matthew 7; 7-8 *Ask and it shall be given you, seek and you shall find knock and it shall be opened unto you. For everyone that asketh receiveth; and he that seeketh findeth and to him that knocketh it shall be opened.*

Charles E. Pratt, Jr.

29.

Attack Your Lack

Attack your lack and tell the devil to get back.

"And from the days of John the Baptist until now, the kingdom of heaven suffereth violence, and the violent take it by force."

Matthew 11; 12

Yes, "Take it by force." Faith at work is the spiritual force that will cause money blessings to flow in your life. You need to get serious, get violent with the devil. Go after what God promised you. Know that what is for you, is for you. God deals in addition and multiplication, while the devil deals in subtraction and division. God wants you to have in abundance. He's called you to have more than enough. It's time out for just barely making it. God has promised to meet all your needs. He just wants you to look to Him and believe. So dare to "Attack your Lack."

"But my God shall supply all your need according to His riches in glory, by Christ Jesus." Philippians 4, 19

God has always met the needs of His people in time of need

..For Israel in the wilderness,

Deuteronomy 2, 7

"For the Lord thy God hath blessed thee in all the works of thy hand: He knoweth thy walking through this great wilderness: These forty years the Lord thy God hath been with thee; thou hast lacked nothing."

For Elijah in the famine

I Kings 17, 6

"And the ravens brought him bread and flesh in the morning, and bread and flesh in the evening; and he drank of the brook."

For the whole army of the three kings

II Kings 3; 20

"And it came to pass in the morning, when the meat offering was offered, that behold, there came water by the way of Edom, and the country was filled with water."

For the widow woman

II Kings 4, 6

"And it came to pass, when the vessels were full, that she said unto her son, bring me yet another vessel, and he said unto her there is not a vessel more and the oil stayed."

..For Samaria in the time of famine

II Kings 7, 8

"And when these lepers came to the uttermost part of the camp, they went into the tent and did eat and drink, and carried thence silver and gold, and raiment and went and hid it, and came again, and entered into another tent, and carried thence also, and went and hid it."

.. For the whole multitude that followed Christ

Matthew 14, 20

And they did all eat, and were filled: and they took up of the fragments that remained twelve baskets full.

You do and God will too!

"Come unto me all ye that labour and are heavy laden, and I will give you rest," Matthew 11, 28

Simply stated; "You come and I will give!"

"But seek ye first the kingdom of God and His righteousness; and all these things shall be added unto you." Matthew 6: 30

Simply stated; "You seek and I will add!"

"Bring ye all the tithes into the store house that there may be meat in mine house and prove me now herewith, saith the Lord of hosts, If I will not open you the widows of heaven, and pour you out a blessing, that there shall not be room enough to receive it." Malachi 3; 10

Simply stated; "You bring and I will pour."

Withdrawals of money from heavens bank are

predicated on the fact of faith. You do and God will too! You come and He, God will give. You seek and He, God will add. You bring and He, God will pour.

Gold in the Mail Box

I remember not so very long ago, when our church building needed a new roof. Water would leak in at the least rain storm, and we lacked the funds to get the job done. So, we began to ask in faith that the money would rain in. In other words, we went fishing. The next day, I found a large manila envelope in the church mail box; inside a small note and a BIG HEAVY GOLD CROSS (14 caret gold).

 The note read, "From a friend, "Thought maybe this would help you in putting a new roof on your building." Yes, God put gold in our mail box, and we were able to get the roof fixed. He allows these types of miracles that we might truly know. *He is a present help in time of trouble.* Psalms 46, 1

Money at the Gas Pump

One mid-spring evening, when I was driving my car on empty, I said to the Lord, "I need a little help." I didn't have but a few dollars to my name. I pulled into the *Cumberland Farm's* Station. I got out of the car and there to my wondering eyes did appear, a giant wade of bills. Yes, on the ground, in front of the gas pump, at my feet, a money miracle, waiting to be picked up. The old song says, "He may not come when you want Him to, but He always comes on time." God knows our need and He's willing, and ready to supply the need. But, He wants you to ask. Ask in faith believing

Ask and it shall be given you, seek and ye shall find. Matthew 7; 7

"Yet, ye have not, because ye ask not. Ye ask, and receive not, because ye ask amiss, that ye may consume it upon your lust." James 4; 2, 3

Ask out of an honest and sincere heart. Ask for kingdom things, that will be a blessing toward the will and purpose of God. Be assured that God will hear and answer your prayer.

Gold At the Door

They had booked me for a revival in Hubbard, Ohio. Hubbard is a quaint little town right outside of Youngstown. I left Pittsfield, Massachusetts, traveling on the Amtrak train. When I arrived in Youngstown that Sunday, morning, I met one of the worst snow storms ever. I got settled into a motel, and due to the blizzard, they had to postpone church services. The next day, when I opened the door at the motel, I saw something shiny under the ice, just in front of the doormat. I started digging it out, and discovered a gold chain. The inscription read 14 caret gold. Again, God had put gold at my feet. I took that chain to a jeweler down that same street and exchanged it for a wonderful sum of cash.

Watch Provided

I will never forget the miracle watch the Lord provided for me in a place called Savant Lake, Ontario, Canada. Savant Lake is located way north in Ontario. The settlement has Cree Indians, lumberjacks, and men who work on the railroads, and highways.

I was there conducting a few nights of revival, with the native people. I had come in by rail, and was scheduled to leave by rail. The train for my departure was leaving at 3 am.

The temperature outside was 30 below 0. This was the normal for winter up there. I realized that I didn't have a watch, and I desperately needed one so I could meet the train at 3 am. I did not want to be out there any longer than necessary. I prayed, "God I need a watch! Thank you for meeting my need."

I was staying in the town's only motel, a place frequented mostly by lumberjacks and highway workers. Shower and bathroom facilities were down the hall in one big community type room. When I went into the bathroom, I discovered a brand new **Luchen Picard** gold watch French and English. I found out that miracles don't just happen, but they are planned. Some how, that timepiece had been planted there just for me.

God has a plan, a purpose and a place for your time, talent and treasure, He wants you to work your faith!

Compulsive Behavior

A type of compulsive behaving

To have and to hold

To tally and fold

Bank notes we crumble and twist

Money's on top of our list

That dynamic craving for saving

A type of compulsive behaving

The fear of going broke

And having a stroke

A type of compulsive behaving

Exorbitant

From moment to moment to moment

The pressures of life are exorbitant

For shelter, for food, and for fuel

For clothing, for health and for school

We wrestle, we work, and we duel

Money divides us into classes

Some cannot grasp, some cannot clasp

Grasping, clasping trying to hold

Seeking, reeking, trying to mold

Ranks of the rich, ranks of the poor

Money deciding who comes in the door.

Faith Is

Faith is the invisible that brings the visible into being.

Faith is the something that takes the nothing and turns it into something.

Faith is the text, the context and the total content for contentment.

Faith is the major factor in obtaining satisfaction.

Faith is the wealth and the wherewithal for all in all.

Faith is the evidence for all in existence.

Faith is the fact that faith works.

Faith is the difference between the talk and the walk.

Faith is the joining of believing with receiving.

Faith is the more than theorizing, prognostic-zing, and generalizing, mystic-zing, and compromising. specializing, **but** knowing that you know that you know.

Faith is the phenomenal fact, that when in tack will attack your lack.

Faith is the unquestioning of belief **not** the fabricating of belief.

Faith is the fact of what God has made. Not the fabric of what man has made up.

Which Do You Want

When it comes to money,

Which do you want?

One is a giver.

The other a taker.

One is a maker.

The other a breaker.

One is so blessed.

The other so distressed.

One is achieving.

The other deceiving.

One is a winner .

The other a sinner.

When it comes to money,

Which do you want?

For Money

For money

Your precious time you gave.

For money

You fuss and fight and rave.

For money

You crave and misbehave.

For money

You slave and try to save.

For money

You work until you cave.

For money

You get into a wave.

For money

You pave an early grave.

Money Makes

Money makes the miser mean
Causing him to act obscene

Money makes the wiser keen
Causing him to act serene

Money makes the poorer scowl
Causing him to act denial

Money makes the richer smile
Causing him to act a while

Money makes the fearer balk
Causing him to act in shock

Money makes the freer stalk

Causing him to act unfrock

Money makes the stealer walk

Causing him to act a hawk

Money makes the liar talk

Causing him to act a mock.

Charles E. Pratt, Jr.

Find Your 'Niche'

Find a place where you can pray
Success will surely come your way

Find a place where you can think
Write your thoughts with pen and ink

Find your NICHE' where you get rich
Act in faith and make a switch

Find your strength and don't delay
Trusting God will always pay.

~~~~~~~~

Building A Nest Egg

Collectors call and speak abrupt

When unpaid bills start piling up

We parlay each day to set a peg

When building on our own nest egg

We borrow to buy when costs are high

And cash receipts are nowhere nigh

We worry and fret with credit debt

And cross our fingers as to bet

We tend to fold and cash our chips

And go to bed with poked out lips.

Charles E. Pratt, Jr.

On Paying Tithes

Every man's giving proportion

   just the same.

Tithes isn't some kind of

   Church rip-off money game.

But a sacred holy truth

   From our blessed Bible,

So to disobey and discount

   You are surely liable.

Give to God that tenth,

   It's already His own.

It can be the greatest fraction

   You've ever known

God has commanded; "Pay your tithes first."

Don't put self first; giving God your worst.

Tithing was not just for men under the law.

But sanctioned today for the ministry to draw,

Sure blessing from tithing, the Lord God has said,

He'll open heaven's windows, so lift up your head.

Give and it shall be given unto you.

Bless and you shall be blessed in all that you do.

So pay your tithes with a cheerful heart,

And the Lord will prosper whatsoever you start.

Invest in the Church

To acquire your dream and desire
Don't look to
a broker or buyer

If you want to get out of the lurch
Start putting your money in church

When you learn to give to the Lord
Your money you no longer horde

~~~~~~~

Money

Money, a means of everyday exchange

Makes some folks act so strange

Giving them a sense of security

Though their motives, *lack of purity*

Living as though nobody else counts

Gold is all important ounce for ounce

Buying, selling, making a gain

But to help the helpless puts them at a strain.

~~~~~~~

Giving

Advance on the fruit of your living
Find the Lord's blessing in giving.

When you give you magnify Christ.

Why fear to make sacrifice?

You create a power reaction,

With only a ten percent fraction.

So get off the black list.

Pay your tithes as a practice.

Giving is a type of the leaven,

That opens up into God's heaven.

You can have what you want.

You can stand up and flaunt.

When, you magnify Christ by your

Giving.

For the Love of Money

For the love of money and what it will buy

We entertain extortion

And many men die.

For material things like fancy fine cars,

And billions we spend

On rockets to Mars.

Building in space the instruments of war

Sadness, heartache, distress

And sorrow sore.

Blinded in the blight of human self-greed

We turn away from our

Fellow man's need.

While the cost of living continues to rise

Making a total wreck of poor men's lives.

Money makes millionaires fortunes go around

The lack of it brings poor men further down

Down, further down on the slum side of town

Without money, there's no food on your table

Without money there's no clothes on our back

Money determines our cast or class label

In accordance with abundance or the lack

To buy, to sell, to get, to gain,

We work, we sweat, we fret, we strain.

Buy from the Lord, gold tried in the fire

Seek spiritual things, like souls for your hire

And elevate your mind above materialistic things

Forsake this evil, the love of money brings.

8 Powerful Turns on Faith

1) **Faith always takes a positive turn.**

2) **Faith turns a Believer into a Receiver.**

3) **Faith is possessed with the determination to be blessed.**

4) **Faith has the will to climb any hill.**

5) **Faith turns a deficit into a benefit.**

6) **Faith banishes fear and comes out in the clear.**

7) **Faith alleviates stress and finds success.**

8) **Faith produces applications in life's pressing situations.**

Thoughts \ Reflections

It is over dessert that we want to desert, because pastry and pie got us into debt.

Save a penny, and soon you'll have many.

He, who goes to borrow, might well end up in sorrow.*

A greedy man will rob himself. **

Advertisement said, "Buy," but your bank account says, "Don't buy!" **

He who spends more money than he would, will never have money to spend when he should.

If we don't deal with money, then money will deal with us. **

Put it in its proper position and you'll find the proper proportion. **

Faith is a type of "debonair," you may not have a dime in your pocket, but you're a millionaire. **

Possess your possessions, or your possessions will possess you.

Today, bankers are going bankrupt, banks are going belly up, and Wall Street brokers are going broke.

~~~~~~~

Work makes money

     Leisure spends it.

When money speaks,

     Truth becomes dumb.

When money argues,

     Eloquence becomes weak.

Charles E. Pratt, Jr.

30.

Conclusion

"In the beginning God created the heaven and the earth." **Genesis 1:1**

Genesis one and one has to be the perfect personification of 'Faith.' The embodiment of perfect working faith. The greatest type and example of an ultimate faith begins and ends with God. No wonder it says *"In the beginning God"* Genesis 1, 1

And the earth was without form, and void; and darkness was upon the face of the deep, and the Spirit of God moved upon the face of the waters. And God said - faith rises above the realm of sight....*Looking unto Jesus, author and finisher of our faith.*" Hebrews 12, 2

Let me say it in legal terms, the world was created by the 'Fiat' of God. 'Fiat-' an order issued by legal authority. The Romans and the Greeks would slam the gavel down, and say "So let it be said, so let it be done." A decree was therefore a decree that could not be revoked; the power of the spoken word.

God speaks and it's good. That which was not becomes that which is. I reject any other explanation or theory of the worlds origin. What was not cannot explain what is, no, nature does not and cannot explain itself. So that what is seen hath not been made out of things which do appear. The spoken Word of God is the source of everything. "Faith, faith, faith just a little bit of faith," we used to sing, " It was faith that enabled Able," so he offered a better sacrifice than Cain. Faith will take you from a life of vice to a life of virtue. Faith brings the unseen into existence therefore, faith is the essence of what we desire within God's promises, the writer says in Hebrews, *"The substance of things hoped for the evidence of things not seen."* Hebrews 11; 1

Here Paul not only defines faith, but he also describes faith. He tells us what faith is as well as what faith does. Faith hopes for, and then brings forth into existence that for which we believe God for. Faith gives substance to hope. So we do not believe in vain, from our firm conviction comes evidence. Faith proves the promise, in spite of the problems. Yes, faith beyond the circumstances, faith beyond the present moment. From the problem to the promise! God rewards the believer. Faith is mandatory in our approach to God. *"But without faith it is impossible to please Him."* Hebrews 11; 6

Faith works to take you to the next level, to the next miracle, but you have to let it work. "Faith in test and faith in time kills trouble all the time." *"But let patience have her perfect work, that ye may be perfect and entire, wanting nothing."* James 1; 4

"By whom also we have access by faith,"... Romans 5; 2

"But that on the good ground are they, which in an honest and good heart having heard the Word keep it, and bring forth fruit with patience." Luke 8; 15

You can be pitiful or powerful so let faith take you from being powerless to being powerful. Stand on the Word, give it some time and thank God in advance for the victory. ***"Victory is mine, victory is mine I told Satan get thee behind victory today is mine!"***

Faith Works

More Publications

By

Charles E. Pratt, jr.

A Pound of Cure

Don't Worry

Education/ Salvation

Forgiveness

I'm Reminded of a Story

Love Is

Moving Forward

Pratt's Practicals

Pratt's Poetry

Thoughts For Christian Living

To Cope With Fear

To Serve the Lord

Winter's Cold